Designed by Charlie Webster

First edition for the United States, the Philippines, and Puerto
Rico, published 1997 by Barron's Educational Series, Inc.

Text © HarperCollins Publishers Ltd 1996

Illustrations © HarperCollins Publishers Ltd 1996

Published by arrangement with HarperCollins Publishers Ltd

All inquiries should be addressed to:
Barron's Educational Series, Inc.
250 Wireless Boulevard
Hauppauge, New York 11788

ISBN 0-7641-5017-0

Library of Congress Catalog Card Number: 96-86135

Printed in Hong Kong
987654321

Farm
Animals

CONTENTS

Down on the Farm

If you have ever visited a farm, you'll know that they are busy places. Farmers have lots of different animals to look after. Horses need grooming, cows need milking, sheep need shearing, and pigs need mucking out.

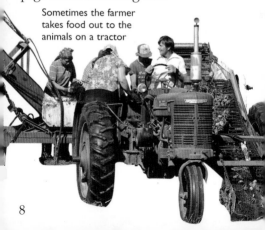

Sometimes the farmer takes food out to the animals on a tractor

A farmyard isn't always this peaceful!

Then there are the chickens, ducks, turkeys, and geese wandering around in the farmyard, waiting to be fed. Farmers have to make sure each one of their animals is healthy and safe all year round.

CHICKENS

A farmyard just wouldn't seem complete without the cock-a-doodle-doo of a proud cockerel. The cockerel is also known as a rooster. He can be recognized by

Leghorn cockerel

Lobe

Coxcomb

Wattle

Rhode Island Red

his colorful feathers and the distinctive red crest on his head, known as the coxcomb. Cockerels can be quite aggressive birds.

Long tail feathers

Belgian Bearded Bantam

Leg feathers

11

CHICKENS

Hens can lay one egg every day throughout the year. If the mother hen mates with a cockerel, chicks will hatch from her eggs about three weeks after she has laid them. The mother hen must sit on her clutch of eggs to keep them warm, and allow the chicks to grow inside.

Silkie chickens are usually white

When a chick is ready to hatch, it pecks through the eggshell with its beak.
Chicks stay close to their mother when they are young.

13

TURKEYS

A male turkey is called a stag

Turkeys on the farm are descended from wild turkeys that lived in the tropical forests of Mexico. Farm turkeys are often so fat that they can't even fly!

The American Mammoth Bronze turkey is the largest of the farm breeds and is now popular all over

the world. The biggest turkey on record was called Tyson. He weighed in at 86 pounds (39 kg) – that's probably more than you!

A male Buff turkey has deep golden feathers

15

DUCKS

Ducks are water birds. Their
webbed feet help them swim and
their beaks (called bills) are handy
for sifting food from pond water. If
there isn't a pond around, ducks
will make do
with puddles
and ditches for

A Muscovy
duck always
has a knob of
red on its bill

splashing their feathers. If you
have ever seen a duck's waddle,
you'll know that webbed feet are
better for swimming than walking!

A pair of
Aylesbury
ducks

Ducks can be reared for their meat
and eggs, but many farmers keep
a family of ducks just because
they're fun to have around.

GEESE

Geese are very big noisy birds. They may not look like guard dogs, but geese will honk fiercely at intruders and chase after them, flapping their wings and hissing!

These Embden geese are snowy white with orange beaks, legs, and feet

Long ago, roast goose was served for Christmas dinner. Goose fairs were held where farmers could bring their birds to market. In the winter months, country people used to rub goosefat over their bodies to keep out the cold.

Baby geese are called goslings

HORSES

Before the invention of modern farm machinery, farmers needed strong horses to help with the back-breaking work. Sturdy farm horses were used for pulling plows or carts full of grain. Even today,

Shire horses

horses are very
useful to have on
a farm, especially
on huge cattle
ranches and
sheep stations.
Farm horses
can live to a ripe
old age and they
need to be well
cared for.
Horses sleep
in stables in the
farmyard and should
have a paddock where
they can graze when
they are "off duty."

DONKEYS

Donkeys have been helping
farmers in all parts of the world for
thousands of years. The ancient
Egyptians were probably the first
people to domesticate donkeys.
Donkeys are
gentle and very
willing workers.
They are perfect
for working on hill
farms because they
are so surefooted.

Donkeys are
smaller than
horses and have
longer ears

A female donkey is called a mare
and her baby is called a foal

Donkeys are often kept as farm
pets. They are intelligent, and
some people will tell you that
they even have a sense of humor
(a donkey's loud bray *does* sound
like a laugh)!

23

COWS AND BULLS

Most of the cows you see on a farm will probably look like these black-and-white calves. They are called Friesians and they are named after the part of Holland where they come from.

Friesian calves

Dairy cows have to be milked twice a day — early in the morning and late in the afternoon

Most dairy cows produce about 6.6 gallons (25 L) of milk every day.

Jersey cows originally came from the Channel Islands in Great Britain. They give us rich creamy milk that can

Jersey cows are cream or golden in color and have very long eyelashes

be made into delicious ice cream.
A good Jersey cow produces up to
ten times her own weight in milk
each year. In the summer, dairy
cows graze out in the fields. They
need to eat plenty of fresh grass.
During the winter months, cows
are fed hay, silage, and cereals.

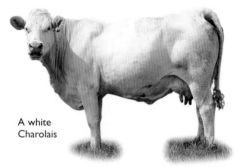

A white
Charolais

Beef cattle are reared for their meat
and have a chunkier build than
dairy cows. In a beef cattle herd
there will be both male bulls and
female heifers. (Heifers are young
cows that have had only one calf.)
In France, the Charolais is the most
popular beef cattle breed.

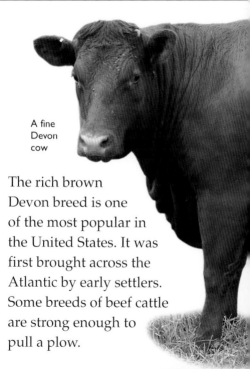

A fine
Devon
cow

The rich brown
Devon breed is one
of the most popular in
the United States. It was
first brought across the
Atlantic by early settlers.
Some breeds of beef cattle
are strong enough to
pull a plow.

COWS AND BULLS

You're quite safe walking through a field of cows, but don't get too close to a bull! When he is nearly one year old, a bull that is going to

A Hereford bull can be recognized by his white face

A Highland bull has a distinctive shaggy coat and long horns

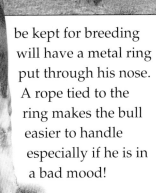

be kept for breeding will have a metal ring put through his nose. A rope tied to the ring makes the bull easier to handle especially if he is in a bad mood!

31

Oxen and Buffaloes

An ox pulling a plow on a farm in the Philippines

In the world's poorer countries, people cannot afford expensive farm machinery. They use strong oxen to pull plows.

Buffaloes provide milk, cheese, meat, and leather for people living in Africa and Asia.

A water buffalo wallowing in a muddy lake

The water buffalo is quite happy helping farmers plow flooded rice fields.

An African buffalo

PIGS

The first people to rear pigs were the ancient Chinese in 1100 B.C. The breeds that we know today have been around for only about 250 years. One of the most popular farm breeds is the Large White. This pig is actually pink and has a cute little curly tail.

Little piglets are always hungry

When fully grown, Large White pigs can weigh up to 440 pounds (200 kg). The mother pig, called a sow, usually has 8 to 12 squealing piglets, and it's a full-time job feeding them all!

A Large White sow with her litter

35

Not all pigs are pink! Just take a look at these beauties. They are Saddleback pigs and they have black patches and huge floppy ears. Like the Large White, the Saddleback can grow to a huge size. But the heaviest pig on record was a Poland-China pig called Big Bill.

In 1933 he weighed 2546.5 pounds (1157.5 kg), was more than 4.9 feet (1.5 m) tall, and measured 9 feet (2.74 m) from nose to tail! Big Bill had to be put down after breaking his leg.

A Saddleback sow with two of her piglets

PIGS

In the past, country people often kept a pig that lived in a stone pigsty next to the house. It was fattened on kitchen scraps and then killed to provide meat for the family.

The Gloucester Old Spot
is an old-fashioned
hardy breed

Some pigs are still kept in brick pigsties where they have a food trough and plenty of straw for a comfortable night's sleep

On some farms, pigs live outdoors. They each have a straw-filled corrugated iron shelter to sleep in at night, but during the day they come out into the field and sniff around for food that they dig up with their snouts. More often, pigs are reared inside large, heated pig houses.

Pigs are friendly creatures, so it is not surprising that certain breeds – like the Vietnamese Potbelly and the Sandy and Black – can be kept as farmyard pets.

Vietnamese Potbelly pigs have wrinkled snouts

A Sandy and
Black sow

Not only are pigs sometimes kept
as pets, they can even be trained!
In France, people use pigs to hunt
for truffles that grow underground.
Truffles are a kind of fungus that
are very tasty and cost a fortune.

41

SHEEP

Swaledale sheep

Sheep are hardy animals and they roam over wide areas on the farm. With their woolly coats, sheep can withstand cold weather. They can survive when food is scarce. There are over 50 different breeds of sheep for farmers to choose from. Sheep are kept for their wool, meat, and milk.

Herdwick sheep come from northern England

A ram (male sheep) with curly horns

SHEEP

The male sheep is called a ram, the female a ewe. Ewes have their lambs early in the spring, often while there is still snow on the ground. At lambing time, many farmers bring their sheep indoors

Two Suffolk ewes, one with her lamb

Lambs drink milk – either from their mother or from a bottle – until they are about 14 weeks old

where they can keep an eye on them all the time. If a ewe dies, her orphan lambs have to be reared by hand. They need to be bottle-fed every four hours – day and night – for the first four or five days.

Sheep shearing takes place once a
year, usually at the beginning of
the summer. It used to be done by
hand and took a long time. Now
electric clippers are used and an
expert can shear 300 sheep in a day.

Shearing is painless for the sheep, and afterwards they have to be dipped to protect them against diseases. The finest quality fleeces come from Merino sheep. Originally bred in Spain, Merinos are now reared mostly on huge sheep stations in Australia.

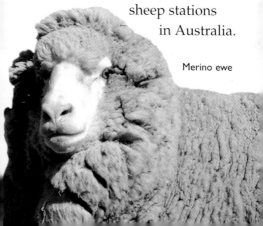

Merino ewe

SHEEP

If you have ever seen a strange-looking sheep on a farm, it probably belongs to one of the "rare" breeds. Jacob sheep are an ancient breed. The lambs have unusual "piebald" fleeces, covered in black and white patches.

A family of Jacob sheep

Soay sheep have
curly coats

As the sheep get older, the black
patches fade to brown.

Another rare breed is the Soay
sheep that comes from
islands off the west coast of
Scotland. It actually looks
more like a goat and its
woolly coat doesn't need
shearing as it molts naturally
in the summer.

SHEEPDOGS

When sheep need to be brought down to the farm for lambing, dipping, marking, or shearing, the farmer rounds them up with the help of a well-trained sheepdog. The dog learns to understand the farmer's commands that are given as shouts and whistles.

An alert
border collie
ready for work

A farmer and his dog rounding up sheep

Collies are among the best
sheepdogs; they are intelligent,
quick, and hard-working. They
know how to control the sheep
without alarming the flock.
Farmers are often proud of their
dogs and take them to sheepdog
trials where they compete in
rounding up sheep or herding
them through narrow gates.

51

GOATS

Goats don't need lush pasture; they'll nibble almost anything, including thorny bushes and prickly plants. If you stand too close to a goat, you may even find that it starts chomping at your clothes! Female goats – called nanny goats – are good milk producers. Some people prefer the flavor of goats' milk, which can be made into rich cheese and yogurt.

A Saanen billy goat showing off his beard

The male billy goats have a distinctive beard under the chin. Two of the best-known breeds of goat – the Toggenburg and Saanen – come from Switzerland.

Baby goats, called kids, are often born as twins

53

GOATS

Many goats are able to survive in dry, hot countries, eating whatever plants they can find. The Nubian goat lives in the deserts of Africa. In the 19th century, it was taken to Britain for breeding. The result was this cute-looking Anglo-Nubian goat, with its long floppy ears and a dappled coat in shades of brown and gray. Today the Anglo-Nubian is the most popular goat in the United States.

An Anglo-Nubian goat having a good chew!

GOATS

The Angora is a small goat with floppy ears that comes from the mountains of Turkey. It is famous for its silky fleece that can be spun into soft mohair wool. All breeds of goat have a soft down that grows under their outer coats.

An Angora goat with its enviable fleece

The best cashmere comes from these Kashmir goats

This fine down is called cashmere and it grows thickest on goats that live in cold places. Cashmere can also be spun into a luxurious wool.

UNUSUAL ANIMALS

You might see some of these unusual animals on a farm near where you live, even though their native countries are far away. Peacocks

A male peacock displaying his fine feathers

are not often eaten, but people like them for their decorative feathers. Ostriches are also kept for their feathers, as well as for their meat and eggs.

Ostrich eggs are the biggest in the world

People living in the mountains of South America have long depended on llamas for food, wool, and transport.

Llamas are related to camels

Now these animals are farmed in other parts of the world for their long fine wool. Llamas can be stubborn and bad-tempered!

INDEX